MONEY BASICS

LIVING ON A BUDGET

by Emma Huddleston

BrightPoint Press

San Diego, CA

BrightP◊int Press

© 2020 BrightPoint Press
an imprint of ReferencePoint Press, Inc.
Printed in the United States

For more information, contact:
BrightPoint Press
PO Box 27779
San Diego, CA 92198
www.BrightPointPress.com

LIBRARY OF CONGRESS CATALOGING-IN-PUBLICATION DATA

Names: Huddleston, Emma, author.
Title: Living on a budget / by Emma Huddleston.
Description: San Diego, CA : ReferencePoint Press, [2020] | Series: Money basics | Includes
    bibliographical references and index. | Audience: Grades 10-12.
Identifiers: LCCN 2019034010 (print) | LCCN 2019034011 (eBook) | ISBN 9781682827970
    (hardcover) | ISBN 9781682827987 (eBook)
Subjects: LCSH: Budgets, Personal--Juvenile literature. | Finance, Personal--Juvenile
    literature.
Classification: LCC HG179 .H833 2020 (print) | LCC HG179 (eBook) | DDC 332.024--dc23
LC record available at https://lccn.loc.gov/2019034010
LC eBook record available at https://lccn.loc.gov/2019034011

CONTENTS

WHAT IS A BUDGET?

Abby wipes away sweat. She is working as a server. The restaurant is hot. She picks up two plates. She brings them to people. She cleans off another table. The people who ate there left a tip. She puts the extra dollars and coins in her pocket. She is saving for prom. Each dollar counts. If she makes enough money, she

Budgets are helpful for anyone who has money.

will get her nails done. Otherwise, she will paint them herself.

Abby uses a budget. A budget is a tool for keeping track of money. Budgets have two parts. One part shows how much

Clothing is a need. But expensive clothing is a want.

money she makes. The other shows where her money goes. Abby's budget helps her track spending. She thinks of her father's advice. He said, "Remember the first rule of budgeting: don't spend money you don't have."

Budgets balance the cost of wants and needs. Wants are costs that a person doesn't need to live. They include fun items or entertainment. Needs help people survive. Those costs include food and shelter. Abby's budget helps her spend carefully. She separates her wants from her needs.

Right now, her parents pay for her needs. Abby could spend all her money on wants. But she doesn't. She focuses on saving money. She can use it in the future. Prom is her short-term goal. Getting her nails done will be a reward. She can treat herself for following her budget. Her long-term goal is college tuition. She is saving for her education. She adds a little money from each paycheck. Over time, the money in her bank account grows.

Abby is responsible with her money. Her budget helps her stay on track. She is practicing smart spending before going to college. In college, she will live on her own. She will have to pay for all her wants and needs. She doesn't want to waste her money or accidentally spend too much. Learning how to budget will prepare her for the future.

College is expensive. It is best to start saving early.

CHAPTER ONE

WHY DO PEOPLE NEED BUDGETS?

People use budgets for three main reasons. First, budgets help people pay off debt. Debt is money owed to another person or business. It is important to pay back debt. Second, budgets help people save for goals. Reaching goals feels rewarding. People have big and small goals. They might dream of a bigger house or a

Budgets help people make the most of their money.

certain pair of shoes. People use budgets

to turn dreams into reality. They save

enough money to reach their goals.

Finally, budgets help people control their

money. Responsible people use budgets.

Budgets help them organize the money they

make. They see how their money is used.

Understanding their spending is important.

It can lead to a positive mindset. In 2017,

65 percent of Americans lost sleep because

they were stressed or worried about money.

People are emotionally connected to

WORKING TOGETHER

Money is a huge issue for many people. In 2017, money was the number one cause of relationship stress. Many couples did not agree on how they should spend money. Budgets help people avoid fighting about money. People talk about spending goals. Then they work together to reach those goals. They can also split some money. Each person can spend a certain amount however they want.

their money. Knowing how to handle money helps people relax and enjoy life better.

WHO NEEDS TO BUDGET?

Everyone can benefit from budgeting. A person doesn't need to be good at math. It doesn't matter if he or she already has a job. Budgets are useful even if someone is debt-free or saving for a small goal. Budgets are not just about **restricting** people's spending. They are informative. People use budgets to see where their money is going.

Budgets allow people to live comfortably. Living comfortably means people's needs are met and they get to have fun.

Young people may get an allowance or earn money from doing small jobs. They can begin to budget their money.

Having fun is different for everyone. Some people go on a big vacation once a year. Others like to have fun more often. They can do this in many small ways. Some eat out once a week. Others go shopping or to the movies.

Ultimately, spending money comes down to what people value. What is a **priority** to them? What people value is often shaped by where they live and who they live with. They see different lifestyles. As they grow up, they decide what kind of life they want. This lets them figure out what they want to spend money on.

BUDGET MINDSET

Living on a budget can be challenging. Setting goals takes focus. Careful spending requires discipline. It also takes practice. Experts remind people to "think about how you want your future to be and remember that keeping to your budget will help you get there."[1]

Many people who use budgets think it is worth the effort. They experience a feeling of freedom. They know where their money is going. They are less stressed about paying bills. They enjoy responsibly spending the money they do have.

A budget needs to be balanced. It is balanced if the money left over is zero or more. People check their income. It should be equal to or more than their expenses. If it's not, they might need to update their budget. But no one is perfect. People go off

Budgets can help people feel confident about the money they spend.

track sometimes. They use budgets to take

control again. Experts suggest people make

budgets with wiggle room. Wiggle room

allows them to make mistakes. It is money

set aside in the budget. For most people,

putting $50 to $100 aside each month is enough. This money can cover unexpected costs or go into savings.

SETTING GOALS

Experts agree that budgets work best when they are focused on a goal. One expert says, "You can use [a goal] to drive your entire budget in the direction of success."[2] Goals can range from big to small. They can be about paying back a **loan** or buying a new phone. People with specific goals are more likely to reach them. They don't go off track as easily. They are more focused.

Specific goals answer questions about what, why, and when. What is the goal? Why does the person have the goal? When does the person want the goal to be achieved? People can set deadlines.

STRESS-FREE SPENDING

Zina Kumok said her attitude toward money in high school was "I'll worry about that later." After graduating and going to college, she said, "One of the best gifts you can give yourself in high school is to understand and follow a budget. . . . Learning how to budget now will teach you how to value your paycheck, save for the future and spend money on what makes you happy."

Zina Kumok, "Budgeting Tips to Help You Take Control of Your Money," Knowledge@Wharton High School (blog), The Wharton School, February 19, 2015. https://kwhs.wharton.upenn.edu.

Buying a house is a goal that can take many years to save for.

Deadlines are specific dates when a person wants to have part of the goal done. Deadlines break up the goal. People see progress at each deadline.

Everyone uses money. Therefore, everyone should think about how they spend it. Budgeting is helpful for multiple reasons. Budgets help people make smart decisions. They only spend money on items they care about. People can see budgeting as a chore. Or they can change their mindset and view it as a tool.

CHAPTER TWO

WHAT IS A PERSON'S INCOME?

ncome is money coming in. People earn an income by working. They are paid in exchange for work. There are two main ways people earn money. Some earn hourly wages, and some earn a salary. People who earn hourly wages are paid a set amount per hour. They often work part-time.

People who share an income work together to create a budget.

This means they work less than forty hours a week. Many students work part-time. They spend other parts of their day in class. People who earn a salary are paid a set amount per year. They often work full-time.

This means they work forty hours or more per week.

Some people share an income. They spend money on food or shelter together. For example, couples and families often share. Their income comes from multiple places. More than one person could be working. Together, they pool their income. Pooling means they put all their money together.

UNDERSTANDING INCOME

Gross income is a person's pay before taxes and deductions. Taxes are payments to the government. They help cover public costs such as roads. Roads are used by all people. The government pays to take care of them.

A deduction comes out of a person's gross income. Payments for health and dental insurance are a type of deduction.

DOES EVERYONE PAY TAXES?

All working people must report their income each year. But not everyone pays taxes on income. People pay income taxes if they earn more than a certain amount of money. The amount they pay depends on their age and status. Status options include single, married, head of household, and **widow**. In 2018, single people under age sixty-five had to earn $12,000 or more to pay income taxes. People who earned less did not have to pay income taxes.

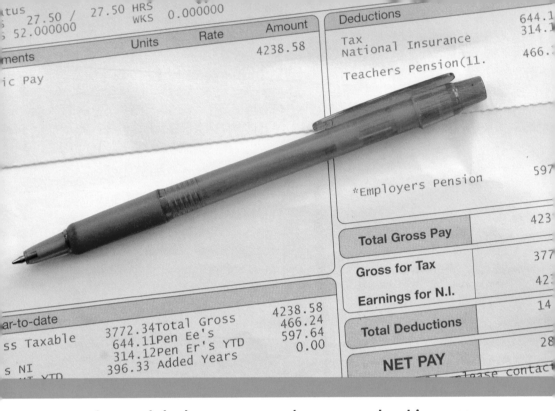

A pay stub shows a person's gross and net income.

So are payments to a retirement account.

Some people may not have insurance

or retirement accounts through their

companies. They would not have

these deductions.

People make budgets based on their

net income. Net income is someone's pay

after taxes and deductions. Sometimes people make extra money. They might help a neighbor with a chore. The neighbor could pay them a small amount. People could win the lottery. Or they might get a **bonus**. Many companies give bonuses to employees who do great work. A bonus is an example of unexpected income. Unexpected income is money someone didn't plan on earning.

When people make budgets, they don't include unexpected money in their total income. They can't count on it. They never know for sure if they will get it. They base their income on their wages or salary.

They can safely rely on this income. Then

they choose what to do with unexpected

money. Some add it to savings. Others

treat themselves with it. They might go to a

nice restaurant.

WHEN SHOULD TEENS START PAYING BILLS?

Some adults believe teens should pay some of
their own bills, such as cell phone bills. Other
adults want to pay for their children. They don't
want to trouble teens with bills. Parents who
pay their teens' bills may need to balance these
payments with other important expenses.
Parents and children should make a plan
together. The plan for paying bills can balance
each side's responsibility.

People may spend money they don't have when they don't budget and track their money.

WHAT ARE A PERSON'S MEANS?

A person's means are the money they

have to spend. Living within your means

is about making smart choices. It is

responsible spending. It looks different

from person to person. Some people can

afford expensive items. They can buy front-row tickets to shows. They can fly to other countries for vacation. Other people have simple means. They drive instead of flying. They shop at thrift stores. They only buy expensive items for special occasions.

Sometimes people live outside their means. They spend too much. They may need to fix their budget. Some experts compare a broken budget to a leaky pipe. They say, "Once you figure out where the money is leaking, you can start plugging the cracks."[3] Budgets help people live within their means.

Living paycheck to paycheck can hurt people's mental health.

LIVING PAYCHECK TO PAYCHECK

Most people have a tight budget. In 2019, a study found that 78 percent of US workers lived paycheck to paycheck. People living paycheck to paycheck have little or no savings. They spend most or all of their

One way to cut expenses is to spend a little less each month. This is easier than cutting a lot at once.

money on needs. They mainly pay for basic expenses. They rely on every paycheck to get by.

Lauren Wellbank and her husband both have jobs. They also live paycheck to paycheck. The Wellbanks use a budget. They carefully plan their spending. Lauren wrote, "We earn enough to put food on the table, and our two small children have everything they need, but some months we barely scrape by."[4] She admitted living within their means was not easy. They were one unexpected expense away from disaster.

A budget can help people stop living paycheck to paycheck. People plan their budgets. They track their spending. They see what expenses they can cut. Over time, they can save money. They don't have to stress about each paycheck.

CHAPTER THREE

WHAT KINDS OF EXPENSES ARE THERE?

E xpense is money flowing out. People's expenses come from multiple places.

Expenses can go into two main categories.

TYPES OF EXPENSES

The first category is fixed expenses. Fixed expenses happen regularly. They are set. People pay the same amount each month.

A payment on a car loan is a fixed expense. The cost of gas is a variable expense.

Big payments such as rent are fixed. The

second category is variable expenses.

Variable expenses change each month.

They go up and down based on people's

decisions. Shopping or eating out are

variable expenses. Someone could spend

more on shopping one month and more on eating out the next.

Variable expenses do not happen regularly. People spend money on birthdays, holidays, and vacations.

LIVING ON ONE INCOME

Josh Monroe and his wife decided to live on one income. Before she quit her job, they tracked expenses. They set lower spending goals. They wanted to be sure they were ready to live on one income. Monroe pointed out how important their budget was. He said, "As you practice living on one income, there may be some lifestyle adjustments. This is why having a firm grasp on fixed and variable expenses is so important."

Josh Monroe, "How to Make the Switch from a Two-Income Household to Just One," CNBC News, *May 8, 2019. www.cnbc.com.*

These events are special. Variable expenses also include unexpected expenses. Unexpected expenses can happen suddenly. People might pay to fix their car after a crash. Sometimes people or their pets become sick or injured. They pay for doctor or veterinarian visits.

HOW DO PEOPLE HANDLE FIXED EXPENSES?

Most fixed expenses are paid monthly. Rent is paid to building owners. **Mortgage** payments go to the bank. Electricity and phone bills go to companies. Loans are paid back to a bank.

Roommates may save money by splitting rent and grocery bills.

One important fixed expense is housing. People need a place to live. Budgets can help them choose the right place. They show what kind of place people can afford. Bigger homes usually cost more. People can save money by getting a smaller place.

Sometimes the cost depends on the location. Moving to certain areas can save money. Living with a roommate can lower costs. Roommates share rent payments. They can also make living in a home more fun.

Housing is a big expense. It can also be a chance to save money. Many people cut costs while decorating. They make their own art for the walls. They don't buy brand new items. They get used furniture. People do their own repairs. They fix leaky sinks. They paint old or scuffed chairs. Doing home projects can be fun and rewarding.

One expert says, "Not only will you save

cash and learn some extremely useful skills,

but you can take pride in your work."[5]

HOW DO PEOPLE CHOOSE VARIABLE EXPENSES?

Variable expenses change. Grocery bills

go up and down. People eat at restaurants

CLIPPING COUPONS

Many stores have coupons. A coupon is exchanged for a special deal on a product. Billions of US shoppers use coupons. Coupons are sometimes called free money. They can be an easy way to save. The drawback is that using them takes time and organization. People look through newspapers and websites to find coupons. They go to multiple stores for certain deals. Sometimes people don't think this work is worth the savings.

Buying a daily cup of coffee can cost around $1,000 a year.

or cook at home. Buying gas for a car

depends on how much someone drives.

Entertainment includes many activities.

Going to a sporting event is expensive.

Playing a board game at home is cheaper.

People watch movies in theaters or at home.

The average cost of a restaurant meal is around $13. The average cost of groceries for a meal is around $4.

Some people shop often. Others rarely spend money on clothes.

Experts encourage people to choose variable expenses carefully. Some costs, such as buying a coffee in the morning, may seem small. But they can add up over time. Variable expenses are not regular or set amounts. People are free to spend as much or as little as they want on them.

One main variable expense is food. People have to eat. But they can be smart about food costs. Some grocery stores are cheaper than others. Certain foods and brands are more expensive. In the United States, the average family of four spends between $710 and $1,100 on food per month. People could make changes to spend less. Experts agree that "eating out often costs more than cooking at home."[6]

Budgeting Expenses

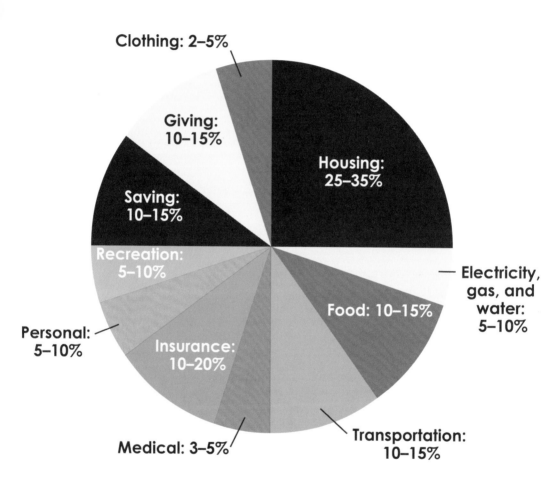

Clothing: 2–5%

Giving: 10–15%

Saving: 10–15%

Recreation: 5–10%

Personal: 5–10%

Insurance: 10–20%

Medical: 3–5%

Housing: 25–35%

Electricity, gas, and water: 5–10%

Food: 10–15%

Transportation: 10–15%

Some people put a certain percentage of their income toward different expenses. The chart above shows a starting point for dividing income among expenses.

People save money buying food in bulk.

They learn valuable skills while cooking.

People save time making meals with few

ingredients. They don't waste time waiting

in restaurants. They don't pay extra to tip

servers or pay for gas to drive there.

Budgets balance income and expenses.

People use budgets to see how money

flows in and out. They keep track of

expenses. Overall, their goal is to spend

less than they earn.

CHAPTER FOUR

HOW DO PEOPLE LIVE WITHIN A BUDGET?

Living within a budget takes practice. It is about focus and goals. People must choose what they want to spend money on. Some focus on saving. They put any extra money they have into savings. Other people focus on spending. They use all of their money. They might enjoy

Budgets help people focus their spending on things that matter to them, such as travel.

fun items. They could buy plane tickets to

travel. They could buy fashionable clothes.

HOW TO SET GOALS

Once a budget has a focus, people set

goals. Their goals should be realistic.

People need a plan to pay off debt. Making a budget is part of that plan.

Realistic goals are not too high. A big goal is often reached over time. People set aside small amounts of money until they reach it.

Sarah McGowan paid off more than $36,000 in student loans in less than two years. She worked multiple part-time jobs.

WHAT ABOUT DEBT?

Many people have some form of debt. They may have a mortgage to pay off. They may have car loans or student loans. People can use budgets to organize their debt payments. One way to pay off debt is by paying late bills first. Another way is by paying small debts first. People make a list of all debts. They pay certain amounts to each one every month. Once the smallest debt is taken care of, they use its payments for the bigger debts. Eventually all the debts are paid for.

She budgeted carefully. She tried to not spend extra money. She said, "I tried really hard to keep a grateful mindset and to focus on what I did have instead of what I didn't have. I wanted to get rid of the debt."[7]

TWO COMMON TYPES OF BUDGETS

Dave Ramsey is a radio show host. He gives people money advice. Ramsey recommends the zero-based budget. Every dollar is divided between saving and spending. It helps people avoid debt. It helped Ramsey become a millionaire. Elizabeth Warren is a US Senator from Massachusetts. She created the 50-30-20 budget. This budget divides a person's income. A person can spend 50 percent on needs, 30 percent on wants, and 20 percent on savings.

WHAT METHOD IS RIGHT FOR YOU?

After people choose a focus and their goals, they can choose a budget type. Different types of budgets divide money in different ways. Some types are best for spending. Others help people save. People can reach different goals depending on the type of budget they follow.

People use different methods to make budgets. Many create budgets on their own. Some pay professionals to help them. People can check their budgets weekly or monthly. Different methods help people budget successfully. There's no right or

People can find budget spreadsheets online, or they can create their own.

wrong way to budget. The point is finding

what works best for a person's situation.

TYPES OF BUDGETS

Many people use spreadsheets. A

spreadsheet is a grid. The grid is made of

many small boxes. The boxes form columns
and rows. People can write spreadsheets
on paper. Or they can use a spreadsheet
computer program. They list their income
in one row. They list expenses in another.
Then they add up both rows. They subtract
their expenses from their income. The
spreadsheet clearly organizes the numbers.
It shows whether people have enough
money to cover their expenses. People can
easily see how their money flows in and out.

Some people use the envelope method.
This method works well for people who
often use cash. It is also good for people

who like to physically handle their money.

First, they gather several envelopes. Then

they label each envelope with an expense.

Common labels are "rent," "phone bill,"

"food," "savings," and "fun." Next, they

write a number value on each envelope.

The number is how much they can spend

on each of those things. The numbers are

based on their budget. Finally, they fill each

envelope with the right amount of cash.

As they use money, they see their budget

working. They notice when envelopes

are full or empty. Wealth management

expert David Mullins thinks setting up the

The envelope method keeps spending in check. Once an envelope is empty, no more money can be spent on that category.

envelopes is the hardest part. This method

gets easier over time. He says, "Do this for a

year, and you will be shocked at how much

easier handling your budget will be."[8]

Budgeting apps let people see their budgets anywhere.

Other budgeting methods include technology. People use websites and **apps**. They create budgets on their computer or smartphone. They enter their income and expenses into the app. The app tracks their spending. It shows money going in and out. People see exact amounts of money. Some apps can even connect to people's bank accounts. The app shows people how much money they have left. People find apps convenient. They can easily see their spending. They can check the app at any time.

CHAPTER FIVE

WHAT ARE SOME BUDGETING TIPS?

P eople change their budgets throughout their lives. They set new goals. Along the way, they create habits. Bad habits need to be broken. Spending too much on fun items is a bad habit. Good habits take practice. Putting money into

Good budgeting habits help people throughout their lives.

savings each month is a good habit. Good

habits lead to success.

No matter what type of budget people

choose, they should try to stick to it. One

expert says, "What seems complicated now

People can save money by buying items that are on sale.

will eventually just become another habit."[9]

Budgeting is a habit worth creating. It can be used during all stages of life.

BUILDING GOOD HABITS

There are many tips people can follow to build good habits. One tip is to check bills and bank records for errors. Sometimes companies make mistakes. They could charge someone too much money.

Another tip is to compare prices. People can compare products made by different brands. They can also compare the same product sold by different stores. Comparing prices makes people aware of costs. People can compare prices for small items at the grocery store. They can also do it for large expenses, such as cars. Comparing prices takes time. People search for deals. They go to more than one store. In the end, extra effort can save them money.

A good habit is paying bills right away. Paying on time is responsible. This habit can also save people money. Companies may charge people for late payments. But some people find it difficult to pay on time. They don't remember how much and when to pay. Automatic payments can make paying bills easy. A company can connect to a person's bank account. The company takes the right amount of money out of the account each month. Many people find automatic payments helpful.

Another good habit is setting goals. Experts have many tips for setting goals.

Those who write down their goals are more likely to reach them.

One tip is making a specific list. People

write down amounts for each goal. For

example, imagine a young man wants

to buy new shoes. They cost $59.99.

He also wants a certain book. It costs $15.99. Knowing how much his goals cost can help him reach them. He sees some choices are better than others. Spending money on a $2.99 soda takes away from his goal. He keeps the list somewhere he will see it every day. Some people put their lists on their refrigerators. Others pin them above their desks. Seeing a list each day reminds people of their goals. When they remember what they are saving for, it is easier for them to give up other items.

Another tip is talking to someone about a goal. One expert says, "You can make a pact with a friend to always call her if you're about to make a purchase over $25. . . . If your friends want to go shopping, you only bring $5 in cash so you can't spend any more."[10] People can encourage each other to save money.

THE TWENTY-FOUR-HOUR RULE

One tip for saving money is the twenty-four-hour rule. People wait twenty-four hours before buying an item. They think about whether the item is a want or a need. Then they decide if they still want to spend money on it. They check the budget. Sometimes they look for better deals. Waiting to buy an item helps people avoid quick, unnecessary buys. The rule can save them money.

For big goals, experts suggest small rewards. People can treat themselves each month that they are on track. People enjoy the reward. They also feel motivated to keep going. When they make other sacrifices, it is worth it. They are still looking forward to reaching their goal.

HOW DO BUDGETS HELP PEOPLE SAVE MONEY?

Experts agree saving money is one of the best habits. Savings can pay for unexpected costs. They can also help people reach goals. People save money for different reasons. They save for big payments. Paying for a house or car can cost a lot of money. These costs take months or years to save for. Additionally, people save for retirement. Retired people no longer work. But they still need money to live.

SAVING FOR RETIREMENT

It is never too early to start saving for retirement. Many people use a Roth IRA account for savings. They pay taxes before adding to it. When they take money out later in life, it is not taxed again. One expert says, "As the old adage goes, the best time to plant a tree was 20 years ago. . . . The earlier [people] can begin to save for their future, the better."

Kyle A. Sanders, "Why Your Children Should Start Saving for Retirement in High School, and How You Can Help," Legacy Consultants Group, *March 19, 2018.* www.legacyconsultantsgroup.com.

Health problems can be expensive. Without health insurance, a trip to the emergency room may cost thousands of dollars.

Sometimes savings are called rainy

day funds. That nickname is about paying

for unfortunate events. Emergencies and

sudden costs can feel like bad luck or a

rainy day. These costs can be expensive.

In 2014, 60 percent of Americans faced

unexpected costs. In 2017, almost 60 percent of Americans had less than $500 in savings. Experts suggest starting with $1,000 in savings. People can save more over time. These savings can help cover unexpected costs.

Many high school students focus their budgets on savings. They are not living on their own. Their parents pay for their needs. They only have to pay for wants. Instead of spending all their money, they put large amounts in savings. Many use savings to buy a car. Others use savings to pay for college.

DO BUDGETS CHANGE OVER TIME?

People's budgets change all the time. Students graduate. Workers get a **promotion**. Families might have to pay for an emergency. Someone might pay off debt or loans. People can accidentally go off track. They may spend too much after getting a higher-paying job. They are not used to making more money. They reward themselves with fun items. And they don't realize how much they spend. For all these reasons, people need to update their budgets often.

Getting a new job can be an exciting life change. People should adjust their budgets with life changes.

Budgeting helps people reach goals big and small. It gives people control over their money. They can plan for the future. They can turn their dreams into reality.

WORKSHEET

To make sure others can use this book, please complete the activity on a separate sheet of paper.

SETTING UP YOUR BUDGET SPREADSHEET

At the beginning of the month, create a budget spreadsheet like the one on the right. In the Income section, list the income that you expect to earn. In the Expenses section, list what you plan to spend your money on. Fill out the Budget column with the amount you want to spend on each item. The total for the Budget column should match the total for the Expected Income column. Try to use exact numbers as much as possible.

Throughout the month, keep track of your income and expenses. Fill out the Actual columns in the Income and Expenses sections. Add them up to get their totals. How did you do? Did you stay within your budget? Or did you spend more than you earned? How can you improve your budget next month?

Budget for the Month of ___June___		
INCOME		
Source	Expected	Actual
Allowance	$40	$40
Mowing the Lawn	$20	$20
Babysitting	$35	$45
Total:	$95	$105
EXPENSES		
Type	Budget	Actual
Savings	$40	$40
Entertainment	$20	$30
Food	$15	$10
Shopping	$20	$20
Total:	$95	$100

GLOSSARY

apps
programs designed for mobile devices

bonus
an extra amount of money given to an employee

loan
money borrowed from a person, bank, or company

mortgage
a type of loan used to buy a house

priority
something that is important to a person

promotion
a raise in position or pay

restricting
limiting or holding back with force

widow
a person whose partner has died

SOURCE NOTES

CHAPTER ONE: WHY DO PEOPLE NEED BUDGETS?

1. Akhilesh Ganti, "Budget," *Investopedia*, June 25, 2019. www.investopedia.com.

2. John Schmoll, "4 Ways to Live on a Budget When You Don't Know Where to Start," *US News*, February 22, 2016. https://au.finance.yahoo.com.

CHAPTER TWO: WHAT IS A PERSON'S INCOME?

3. Latoya Irby, "How to Stop Living Paycheck to Paycheck," *The Balance*, February 6, 2019. www.thebalance.com.

4. Lauren Wellbank, "I Am 37 Years Old and I Live Paycheck to Paycheck," *HuffPost*, December 7, 2018. www.huffpost.com.

CHAPTER THREE: WHAT KINDS OF EXPENSES ARE THERE?

5. Nathan Chandler, "5 Tips for Living Comfortably on a Budget," *HowStuffWorks*, October 10, 2011. https://money.howstuffworks.com.

6. Chandler, "5 Tips for Living Comfortably on a Budget."

CHAPTER FOUR: HOW DO PEOPLE LIVE WITHIN A BUDGET?

7. Quoted in Bev O'Shea, "How I Ditched Debt: 'I Just Pretended I Didn't Have Money,'" *NerdWallet*, July 8, 2019. www.nerdwallet.com.

8. Quoted in Danielle Wiener-Bronner, "How Can I Keep Track of My Money?" *CNNMoney*, June 29, 2017. https://money.cnn.com.

CHAPTER FIVE: WHAT ARE SOME BUDGETING TIPS?

9. Wiener-Bronner, "How Can I Keep Track of My Money?"

10. Zina Kumok, "Budgeting Tips to Help You Take Control of Your Money," *Knowledge@Wharton High School* (blog), *The Wharton School*, February 19, 2015. https://kwhs.wharton.upenn.edu.

FOR FURTHER RESEARCH

BOOKS

Eric Braun and Sandy Donovan, *The Survival Guide for Money Smarts: Earn, Save, Spend, Give*. Golden Valley, MN: Free Spirit Publishing, 2016.

Tammy Gagne, *Paying for College*. San Diego, CA: ReferencePoint Press, 2020.

Cecilia Minden, *Living on a Budget*. Ann Arbor, MI: Cherry Lake Publishing, 2016.

INTERNET SOURCES

Blue Chip Kids, "Budgets in Action," *PBS*, April 26, 2018. www.pbs.org/video.

"Budgeting," *Federal Student Aid*, n.d. https://studentaid.ed.gov.

Katy McWhirter, "Budgeting for College Students," *Affordable Colleges Online*, n.d. www.affordablecollegesonline.org.

"10 Budgeting Tips," *Money 101* (blog), *College in Colorado*, n.d. www.cicmoney101.org.

WEBSITES

Investopedia: Budgeting and Savings
www.investopedia.com

Investopedia's budgeting and savings articles go beyond basic budget questions, with tips for saving on airline tickets and cars.

Mint
www.mint.com

Mint is a free budget tool recommended by many financial experts. It keeps bank accounts, credit cards, and loans all in one place to help make easy budgets.

NerdWallet
www.nerdwallet.com

In addition to budgeting tools and advice (found under the Money tab), NerdWallet features articles on credit cards, loans, and more.

INDEX

IMAGE CREDITS

Cover: © Roman Motizov/Shutterstock Images
5: © SDI Productions/iStockphoto
6: © Vera_Petruninai/iStockphoto
9: © designer491/iStockphoto
11: © BartekSzewczyk/iStockphoto
14: © CGN089/Shutterstock Images
17: © yulkapopkova/iStockphoto
20: © sturti/iStockphoto
23: © katleho Seisa/iStockphoto
26: © Lovattpics/iStockphoto
29: © Chainarong Prasertthai/iStockphoto
31: © urbazon/iStockphoto
32: © pixelheadphoto/iStockphoto
35: © digitalskillet/iStockphoto
38: © monekybusinessimages/iStockphoto
41: © SDI Productions/iStockphoto
42: © Syda Productions/Shutterstock Images
44: © Red Line Editorial
47: © lechatnoir/iStockphoto
48: © Damir Khabirov/iStockphoto
52: © Daniel S. Edwards/Shutterstock Images
55: © Travelsouls/iStockphoto
56: © RichVintage/iStockphoto
59: © Hispanolistic/iStockphoto
60: © fotostorm/iStockphoto
63: © Cn0ra/iStockphoto
68: © mediaphotos/iStockphoto
71: © DMEPhotography/iStockphoto
73: © Red Line Editorial

ABOUT THE AUTHOR

Emma Huddleston lives in the Twin Cities with her husband. She enjoys writing children's books, but she likes reading novels even more. When she is not writing or reading, she likes to stay active by running and swing dancing.